Tell Me Why

WHY?

Poison Ivy Makes Me Itch

Jennifer Colby

Published in the United States of America by Cherry Lake Publishing
Ann Arbor, Michigan
www.cherrylakepublishing.com

Content Adviser: Elizabeth A. Glynn, Youth Education Coordinator, Matthaei Botanical Gardens and
Nichols Arboretum, University of Michigan
Reading Adviser: Marla Conn, ReadAbility, Inc

Photo Credits: © dvande/Shutterstock Images, cover, 1; ©Praisaeng/Shutterstock Images, cover, 1, 15;
©AntonionDiaz/Shutterstock Images, 5; ©Elliotte Rusty Harold/Shutterstock Images, cover, 1, 7;
©carroteater/Shutterstock Images, 9; ©Alila Medical Media/Shutterstock Images, 11; ©wavebreakmedia/
Shutterstock Images, 13; ©Elena Elisseeva/Shutterstock Images, 17; ©NatalieJean/Shutterstock Images,
19; ©Golden Pixels LLC/Shutterstock Images, 21

Library of Congress Cataloging-in-Publication Data

Colby, Jennifer, 1971- author.
 Poison ivy makes me itch / Jennifer Colby.
    pages cm.—(Tell me why)
 Includes index.
  ISBN 978-1-63362-615-7 (hardcover)—ISBN 978-1-63362-795-6 (pdf)—
ISBN 978-1-63362-705-5 (pbk.)—ISBN 978-1-63362-885-4 (ebook)
 1. Poison ivy—Juvenile literature. I. Title. II. Series: Tell me why (Cherry Lake Publishing)

 SB618.P6C65 2015
 581.6'59—dc23   2014049840

Cherry Lake Publishing would like to acknowledge the work of the Partnership for 21st Century Skills.
Please visit *www.p21.org* for more information.

Printed in the United States of America
Corporate Graphics

Table of Contents

Playing in the Backyard

Evan and his best friend, Jake, were playing softball in his backyard. Evan swung his bat and missed. The ball rolled into the bushes.

"I see it!" Evan called. He reached his bare arm through the branches and weeds to get the ball. He tossed the ball back to Jake.

Evan and Jake don't know it yet. But they were just **exposed** to poison ivy.

Poison ivy usually grows in natural areas. But it can also grow in your own backyard.

Poison ivy grows throughout the United States. It can grow as a shrub in the northern states. It can grow as a vine in the East, Midwest, and South. In the spring, it sprouts yellow-green flowers. Sometimes it has green berries that turn off-white in the early fall.

One thing stays the same. Poison ivy always grows with three small **leaflets** on one stem.

Ask an adult to help you find photos of poison ivy online. Knowing what it looks like helps you to avoid it.

Poison ivy has three small green leaflets on one stem. Remember this saying: "Leaves of three, let it be."

The next morning, Evan woke up with red bumps all over his arm. "Mom!" he cried. "My arm is really itchy."

Evan's mom looked at his skin and frowned. "Oh honey! I think you have a **rash** from poison ivy."

She made an appointment for him to see the **dermatologist**.

Most people are allergic to poison ivy, which means they will have an unpleasant physical reaction. Ask your friends and family if they are allergic.

The itchy rash from poison ivy does not happen right away. It starts 12 to 72 hours after touching the plant.

A Trip to the Dermatologist

"That's a rash from poison ivy," the dermatologist agreed. "Like most people, you're allergic to the oil of the plant."

All parts of a poison ivy plant contain an oil called **urushiol**. When skin comes in contact with the oil, a rash can develop.

You can get the rash from anything that comes in contact with the oil. But without the oil, the rash itself is not **contagious**.

Urushiol oil

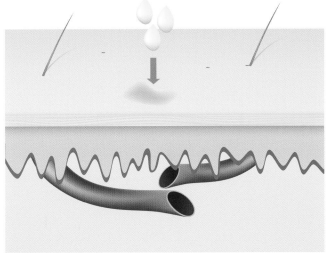

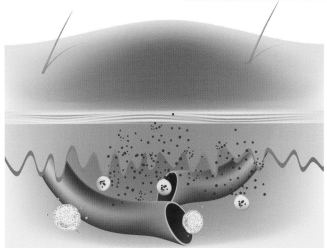

Mild

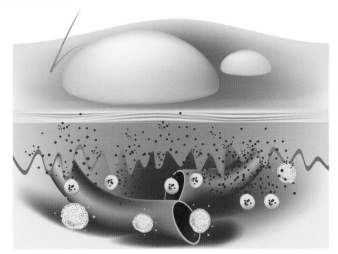

Severe

Urushiol can cause your cells to release a compound.
This produces a rash.

There are three ways to get a rash from poison ivy. **Direct** contact means touching the leaves, stems, roots, flowers, or berries of the plant. **Indirect** contact is if you touch anything that has come in contact with the plant. **Airborne** contact is what happens if you burn the plant, which allows particles of urushiol to land on your skin. Inhaling the smoke can seriously damage your lungs.

Did you touch poison ivy? Or did you touch shoes that walked through poison ivy? Either way, you need to wash with soap and water as soon as possible.

Be careful! You can come in contact with urushiol by petting a dog that has walked in poison ivy.

Treating Poison Ivy

There are many ways to treat a rash from poison ivy. Special lotions can help soothe the skin. Applying a cool **compress** to itchy skin can give you some relief.

Try to leave the blisters alone. Do not scratch them, or they might break open.

Some people have a serious reaction or get an **infection**. Their doctor may give them a **prescription** medicine.

The rash usually goes away in a few weeks.

Evan called Jake as soon as he got home from the dermatologist. "I have a rash from poison ivy. Do you?" Evan asked.

MAKE A GUESS!

How many classmates have had a poison ivy rash? Ask them. Is it fewer students or more students than you had guessed?

A dermatologist may suggest different lotions or using a cool compress to stop the itching.

"Yeah! There's a rash all over my hand!" Jake said. "I don't know how it happened. We didn't play in the woods."

"I remember," Evan said. He explained how the oil from the poison ivy ended up on the ball as they played. "Come on over to my house," he said. "I'll show you where the poison ivy is in the yard."

Poison ivy changes throughout the year. In the spring, it will have flowers. In the fall, it might grow berries.

Avoiding Poison Ivy

Knowing what poison ivy looks like is the best way to avoid getting a rash. Keep your eyes open for plants with three leaves in a cluster. Stay away from them.

Do you walk or play in areas that might contain poison ivy? Keep your skin covered up. Wear long pants, long-sleeved shirts, shoes, long socks, and gloves.

Trail signs often warn against poison ivy.

"Do you see it there under the bushes?" Evan pointed to the poison ivy. "It's the plant with three leaves."

"I see it!" Jake said. "Now that we know what it looks like, we can stay away from it."

Evan and Jake compared rashes. Even though their skin hurt now, they knew it would go away soon.

"Let's play ball," Evan said. "But this time, let's be more careful."

When you spend time outside, keep an eye out for poison ivy and stay away from it.

Think About It!

If a dog or cat walks past poison ivy, it can get urushiol on its fur. If you pet the animal, the oil can get on your skin. Then you might develop a rash. But a dog or cat cannot get a rash from poison ivy. Why do you think that is?

Ask your parents if they've ever had poison ivy. How did it happen? How did they treat it? How long did it take to get better?

Glossary

airborne (AIR-born) moving or being carried through the air

compress (KOM-press) a folded cloth or pad pressed on a body part

contagious (kuhn-TAY-juhs) able to be passed from one person or animal to another by touching

dermatologist (dur-muh-TOL-uh-jist) a doctor who studies the skin and its diseases

direct (duh-REKT) coming straight from a source

exposed (ik-SPOHZD) to be affected by something

indirect (IN-duh-rekt) not going straight from one point to another

infection (in-FEK-shuhn) an illness caused by bacteria or viruses

leaflets (LEEF-lits) small leaves

prescription (pri-SKRIP-shuhn) a written order from a doctor that tells what kind of medicine someone needs

rash (RASH) a group of red spots on the skin caused by an illness or a reaction to something

urushiol (yu-ROO-shee-all) the oil of the poison ivy plant that can cause an allergic reaction

Find Out More

Books:

Lawrence, Ellen. *Poison Petals: Don't Eat!* New York: Bearport Publishing, 2012.

Rhatigan, Joe. *Ouch! The Weird & Wild Ways Your Body Deals with Agonizing Aches, Ferocious Fevers, Lousy Lumps, Crummy Colds, Bothersome Bites, Breaks, Bruises & Burns.* Westminster, MD: Imagine Publishing, 2013.

Web Sites:

KidsHealth—Rashes: The Itchy Truth
http://kidshealth.org/kid/ill_injure/aches/rashes.html
Read about how to treat a poison ivy rash.

North Shore Kid—How to Identify Poison Ivy and Treat Its Rash
http://northshorekid.com/story/how-identify-poison-ivy-and-treat-its-rash
Read about how to treat a poison ivy rash.

Index

About the Author

Jennifer Colby lives in Michigan with her three children. Luckily, she is not allergic to poison ivy. She is a school librarian and loves to help students and teachers find the information they are looking for.